This book is dedicated to our third son,
Thomas, who is our muse....
you will always be our son-shine!

Profiles :
A Dog's Life

Thank you for choosing this book from
Our 3 Sons Publishing.

Want more famous dog
pages sent to your inbox? Use
this QR code for bonus pages.

Members of the Pack:

Napoleon"Bone"aparte

Joan D"Bark"

Benjamin Franklin

Sam Houston

Abraham Lincoln

Cleo"paw"tra

Princess Diana

"Bark" Twain

William Wallace

Davy Crockett

Elvis "Paws"ley

Albert Einstein

Mother Teresa

"Doggy" Parton

King Tutankhamun

Amelia "Ear"hart

"Bow"udicca

Teddy "Ruff"sevelt

Marilyn Monroe

George "Woof"shington

"Drool"ius Caesar

"Bark"beard

Queen Eliza "bark" II

Lud"wag" van Beethoven

Leonardo"dog"Vinci

Sacaga"wag"ea

"Pup" Gregory I

Rosa "Barks"

Winston "Fur"chill

Vincent Van Gogh

William Shakes"paw"

James Earl "Bones"

Marie Antoinette

The Beagles

Napoleon "Bone"aparte

Born: 1769, Corsica
Died: 1821, St. Helena

Napoleon Bonaparte was a French military commander and political leader who rose to prominence during the French Revolution and led many successful war campaigns.

Napoleon had to learn to speak French as a preteen because he grew up in Corsica, which is closer to Italy. He spoke with an Italian accent for the rest of his life.

He was engaged to Désirée Clary, future Queen of Sweden, but broke the engagement when he met the infamous, Josephine.

His actual height was 5 feet 5 inches, which was average height for men of the time.

Napoleon had the *Mona Lisa* hung in his bedroom before the famous painting was moved to the Louvre in Paris.

He finalized the Louisiana Purchase, which doubled the size of the United States, to concentrate his resources in his war against the British.

"Never interrupt your enemy when he
is making a mistake."

Joan D' "Bark"

Born: 1412 France
Died: 1431 Rouen, France

Joan D' Arc is a patron saint of France, and is honored as a defender of the French nation for her role in the siege of Orléans.

Her real name is not actually known. The custom was to take the mother's surname. During her trial, Joan referred to herself only as "Jehanne la Pucelle" ("Joan the Maid")

She is remembered as a fearless warrior and considered a heroine of the Hundred Years' War between France and England, but Joan never actually fought in battle or killed an opponent.

However, Joan was wounded at least twice, taking an arrow to the shoulder during her famed Orléans campaign and a crossbow bolt to the thigh during her failed bid to liberate Paris.

In 1920, Joan of Arc was canonized by the Roman Catholic Church and has been considered a martyr since her death.

"All battles are first won or lost,
in the mind."

Benjamin Franklin

Born: 1706, Boston, Massachusetts
Died: 1790, Philadelphia, Pennsylvania

Ben Franklin was a writer, scientist, inventor, statesman, diplomat, printer, publisher, and political philosopher. Among his many inventions are the lightning rod, bifocals, and the Franklin stove.

At 16, he began writing essays and commentary as widow, "Silence Dogood," and received several marriage proposals from eligible bachelors in Boston.

Franklin is a member of the International Swimming Hall of Fame and had a lifelong love of swimming that began during his childhood in Boston.

Franklin created a phonetic alphabet, where he omitted consonants C, J, Q, W, X and Y and added six new letters, each with its own specific vocal sound.

By 1748, the 42-year-old was rich enough to hang up his printer's apron and became a "gentleman of leisure."

Franklin designed a musical instrument, the glass armonica, used by both Mozart and Beethoven.

"An investment in knowledge pays the best interest."

Sam Houston

Born: 1793, Rock Bridge, Virginia
Died: 1863, Huntsville, Texas

Sam Houston played an important role in the Texas Revolution. He served as the first and third president of the Republic of Texas and was one of the first individuals to represent Texas in the US Senate. He was also the sixth governor of Tennessee and the seventh governor of Texas. He is the only individual to be elected governor of two different states in the United States.

Houston, the city named in his honor was once the capital of Texas.

On April 21, 1836, Houston surprised and defeated Santa Anna and his Mexican army as they camped on the San Jacinto River. Outnumbered by double, Houston's army won in just eighteen minutes.

He became a member of the Cherokee Nation with the given name of, "Black Raven". He married a Cherokee woman and was given a jaguar vest, which he wore to meetings as a Senator in Washington DC.

"Do right and risk the consequences."

Abraham Lincoln

Born: 1809, Hodgenville, Kentucky
Died: 1865, Washington, DC

Abraham Lincoln was the 16th president and used the current Lincoln Bedroom as his personal office. He never slept there but he did meet with Cabinet members and signed documents, including the Emancipation Proclamation.

Lincoln is the only president to hold a patent. His invention was a device for lifting boats in the water.

The Great Emancipator remains the tallest person to serve as president, at 6' 4". He was a gifted storyteller and people loved to gather around to listen to Lincoln's tales and jokes.

He loved animals and reportedly had many pets, including dogs, cats, horses, and even goats.

Abraham Lincoln was an accomplished wrestler as a young man and is in the National Wrestling Hall of Fame in the, "Outstanding American" catagory. He lost only once in approximately 300 matches.

"Nearly all men can stand adversity, but if you want to test a man's character, give him power."

Cleo "paw" tra

Born: 69 BC, Alexandria, Egypt
Died: 30 BC, Alexandria, Egypt

While Cleopatra was born in Egypt, she was not Egyptian. Her family dates to Ptolemy I Soter, one of Alexander the Great's generals, who reigned Egypt after Alexander's death in 323 B.C., and started a dynasty of Macedonian Greece rulers that lasted for over 300 years.

Cleopatra was the first in her line to learn the Egyptian language and she spoke as many as a dozen languages.

She was educated in mathematics, philosophy, oratory and astronomy and some scholars claim that she wrote books on medicine, cosmetics, pharmaceuticals and toxicology, but those were lost over time.

In 48 BC, she wanted to meet the Roman general, Julius Caesar but knew her desires would be stopped by her brother, so she had herself wrapped in a carpet or sack and smuggled into his personal quarters. Caesar was dazzled by the young queen, and the two soon became allies.

Princess Diana

Born: 1961, Sandringham
Died: 1997, Paris

Diana Spencer, Princess of Wales, will always be known as, "the people's princess". She was famous for being a fashion icon and for her humanitarian efforts across the globe.

Diana Spencer had a guinea pig named Peanuts.

She studied ballet and dreamed of taking the stage with the Royal Ballet, but she was too tall.

The princess loved to skate and was photographed roller blading in the Kensington Palace gardens in the 1990s.

Diana walked through a field of landmines in Angola in 1997 to bring awareness to the cause of getting rid of all landmines.

She grew up in a house on the Queen's Sandringham estate. Park House was built during King Edward VII's rein and eventually was passed down to his great-granddaughter Queen Elizabeth. She then in turn rented it to the aristocratic Spencer family.

"I don't go by the rule book, I lead from the heart, not the head."

"Bark" Twain

Born: 1835, Florida, Missouri
Died: 1910, Redding, Connecticut

Samuel Langhorne Clemens was born 2 months prematurely and remained sickly and frail until he was 7 years old.

Clemens' pen name, Mark Twain, came from the steamboat industry. A leadsman would call, "by the mark twain" which meant the river depth was safe for the steamboat.

Twain struck gold in California, but in the literary world. He headed to Calaveras County, California in hopes of striking gold as a prospector (he didn't), but he got inspiration and wrote, *The Celebrated Jumping Frog of Calaveras County*, his first published work.

Twain based Huckleberry Finn on a real person, Tom Blankenship, a boy who was four years older than Twain when he was young. The boy's family was poor and his father, a laborer, had a reputation as a town drunk. Twain said in his autobiography: "In Huckleberry Finn I have drawn Tom Blankenship exactly as he was. He was ignorant, unwashed, insufficiently fed; but he had as good a heart as ever any boy had."

"Continuous improvement is better than delayed perfection."

William Wallace

Born: 1270, Elderslie, Renfrewshire, Kingdom of Scotland
Died: 1305 Smithfield, London, Kingdom of England

William Wallace was a Scottish knight who became one of the main leaders in the wars for Scottish independence.

After the defeat of the English army at the Battle of Stirling Bridge, Sir William Wallace along with Andrew Moray received the appointment as Guardians of Scotland by Scottish nobles. Moray died from injuries sustained in the battle, so that left Wallace as the lone Guardian.

Sir William Wallace was considered a giant for the time, since the average height was just over 5 feet. He was 6 foot 7 inches, with broad shoulders, and had strong arms and legs.

Blind Harry, a 15th century poet, Sir Walter Scott, Robert Burns, and Jane Porter all wrote works featuring Wallace's place in Scottish history.

"Tell your commander that we are not here to make peace but to do battle, defend ourselves and liberate our kingdom."

Davy Crockett

Born: 1786, Limestone, Tennessee
Died: 1836, San Antonio (The Alamo), Texas

David Crockett was a larger-than-life figure of American folklore. He was a frontiersman, politician and historical hero.

He was born in a territory that was almost the state of Franklin which was to be the 14th U.S. state, but failed. It then became an independent republic, but it was eventually reclaimed by North Carolina in 1789. By 1796, the land became part of the newly formed state of Tennessee.

Crockett often made his living as a bear hunter. He spent much of his life stalking black bears in the woods of Tennessee and selling their pelts, meat and oil for profit. He was also a cattle driver for a period of time in his youth.

He helped stop an assassination attempt on Andrew Jackson. As Jackson passed by the crowd, a crazed gunman named Richard Lawrence emerged from the spectators and fired two shots at Jackson. Crockett was one of several bystanders who disarmed the would-be assassin and wrestled him to the ground.

"Remember these words when I am dead.
First be sure you're right, then go ahead."

Elvis "Paw" sley

Born: 1935, Tupelo, Mississippi
Died: 1977, Memphis, Tennessee

Elvis Aaron Presley American popular singer widely known as the, "King of Rock and Roll". Elvis was born approximately 35 minutes after his twin brother, Jesse Garon, who died shortly after. His first record was a gift that he made for his mother when he was just 18 years old.

Elvis served in the Army after he was already famous. He completed advanced military training and served overseas in Germany from 1958-1960.

Elvis once owned a pet chimpanzee named Scatter who made appearances at parties at Graceland to entertain guests.

Even though he was a global music sensation, Elvis never performed live outside of North America.

He was a fan of karate, particularly the fighting style known as Chito-Ryu, even earning his black belt in 1960.

Elvis had an obsession with police and found it entertaining to pose as officers by attaching a siren to his car and then pulling people over as a prank.

"When things go wrong, don't go
with them."

Albert Einstein

Born: 1879, Ulm, Germany
Died: 1955, Princeton, New Jersy

Albert Einstein is considered the smartest scientist to have ever lived and is known for his theory of relativity. A 1919 solar eclipse helped make Einstein world famous, because the sun proved his assertion, "that gravitational fields cause distortions in the fabric of space and time."

He had extremely delayed speech and didn't speak fluently until he was six years old. Einstein also had problems getting his thoughts down, retrieving language and reading out loud, all characteristic signs of dyslexia.

Albert did well in school, especially in maths and sciences. The future Nobel Laureate dropped out of school at age 15 and left Germany to avoid state-mandated military service.

It took Einstein nine years to get a job in academia, probably because of his rebellious personality and habit of skipping class.

He was asked to be the second president of Israel, but declined.

"The more I study science, the more
I believe in God."

Mother Teresa

Born: 1910, Skopje, Republic of Macedonia
Died: 1997, Calcutta, India

At age 18, Agnes Gonxha Bojaxhiu joined the Institute of the Blessed Virgin Mary, known as the Sisters of Loreto, in Ireland and was given the name Mary Teresa. The world called her, "Mother Teresa".

She was a Nobel Peace Prize winner for her work in the struggle to overcome poverty and distress.

In high school, she attended the local church where she joined the sacred heart choir. She was so talented that she was often asked to sing solo verses.

As a teacher on a trip, she heard Christ asking her to go to India and help the poor and sick. After six months of basic medical training, she headed to Calcutta's slums with a single mission to show love to the poor and the sick.

Mother Teresa was fluent in five different languages: Hindi, Bengali, Albanian, English, and Serbian.

"Small things done with great love
will change the world."

"Doggy" Parton

Born: 1945, Sevierville, Tennessee

Dolly Rebecca Parton is the treasure of Tennessee. She is one of twelve siblings and they all lived in a two-room house! Records indicate that Dolly's father paid the doctor who delivered her with either a bag of oatmeal or cornmeal.

At just 13 years old, she performed at the Grand Old Opry for the first time.

Dolly has over 300 wigs and three Guinness Records!

In 2018, Dolly was honored by the Library of Congress because her foundation, Imagination Library, mailed it's 100 millionth book.

She has been married for over 55 years to her husband, Carl. They met at the the Wishy Washy laundromat on the first day she arrived in Nashville.

There is an unreleased song at Dollywood that will be released in 2045, for Dolly's 100th birth year.

"Storms make trees take deeper roots."

King Tutankhamun

Born: c. 1344 BC, Amarna
Died: c. 1327 BC

The, "Boy King" died early, so he was hastily buried in a little known tomb, which might have actually saved his legacy. Tut has the smallest royal tomb in the Valley of the Kings, but he is one of the most famous Pharaohs.

He is much more famous after his death than he was in life because his tomb was found almost completely intact. In November 1922, Howard Carter was the first person in over 3,300 years to see the inside of the tomb. The discovery led to, "Egyptomania" and Ancient Egyptian motifs became a big part of the Art Deco style.

He had a damaged foot and DNA analysis from his mummy shows evidence of multiple malaria infections.

The pharaoh hunted ostriches in the desert east of Heliopolis, according to the inscription on the handle of a feather fan that was discovered in the tomb.

Amelia "Ear"hart

Born: 1897, Atchison, Kansas
Died: ??

Amelia Mary Earhart was the first female aviator to fly solo across the Atlantic Ocean.

She was the aviation editor for Cosmopolitan magazine from 1928-1930.

Earhart received the United States Distinguished Flying Cross, which is a military decoration of the United States Armed Forces.

Amelia was very close friends with First Lady Eleanor Roosevelt. One time, the two snuck out from the White House and went to a party dressed up for the occasion.

Earhart disappeared while attempting to fly around the world with her navigator, Fred Noonan. In a Lockheed Model 10-E Electra, Earhart and Noonan disappeared over the central Pacific Ocean near Howland Island. The two were last seen in Lae, New Guinea, on July 2, 1937.

"As soon as we left the ground,
I knew I had to fly."

"Bow"udicca

Born: 30 AD Camulodunum
Died: 61 AD Battle of Watling Street

Queen Boudicca ruled the Iceni tribe of East Anglia with her husband King Prasutagus. She was a strong female warrior.

"She was very tall, the glance of her eye most fierce; her voice harsh. A great mass of the reddest hair fell down to her hips. Her appearance was terrifying." (Tacitus, Roman historian)

Boudicca and her horde razed the Roman cities of Camulodonum (Colchester), Verulamium (St Albans) and Londinium (London).

Her army met the Romans near Londinium, at the Battle of Watling Street.

Her forces far outnumbered the Roman soldiers, but the terrain created a funnel in battle, which allowed her foe to win easily. She opted for poison instead of being taken as a Roman slave.

Teddy "Ruff"sevelt

Born: 1858, New York
Died: 1919, Cove Neck, New York

Theodore Roosevelt was a politician, statesman, soldier, conservationist, naturalist, historian, and writer who served as the 26th US president. He was also the inspiration for the teddy bear.

Roosevelt was a New York City police commissioner and attempted to reform one of America's most corrupt police departments.

A year after graduation from Harvard, Roosevelt took time from his European honeymoon to scale the Matterhorn with two guides.

Roosevelt was the first president to leave the country, while in office. In 1906, he sailed on the USS Louisiana to personally inspect the construction of the Panama Canal, one of his presidential projects.

Roosevelt authored 38 books. His first book, "The Naval War of 1812", was written at the age of 23 and earned him the reputation of a legitimate historian.

"Knowing what's right doesn't mean much unless you do what's right."

Marilyn Monroe

Born: 1926, Los Angeles, California
Died: 1962, Brentwood, California

Norma Jeane Baker adopted the stage name, Marilyn Monroe, when she got into show business in August of 1946 but she didn't officially change her name until ten years later in 1956.

Marilyn Monroe was such a fan, that she helped Ella Fitzgerald book the Mocambo Club, which propelled Ella's singing career.

Her sheer, spangled dress that she wore to sing "Happy Birthday" to JFK in 1962 sold for over a million dollars. Her white dress worn in, "The Seven Year Itch" sold for 4.6 million!

Joe DiMaggio had roses delivered to her grave twice a week for 20 years following her death.

She worked in the Radioplane factory, an American aviation company that manufactured drone aircrafts during World War II. She met a photographer, who discovered her and introduced her to the world. She was offered film contracts after that.

"Everyone's a star and deserves the right to twinkle."

George "Woof"shington

Born: 1732, Pope's Creek, Virginia
Died: 1799, Mount Vernon, Virginia

George Washington was the first president of the United States but he never lived in the White House. He was unanimously elected president, two times!

His family arrived in America in 1657, on a ship called, *The Sea Horse of London*. When he was born, he was not given a middle name.

He was an excellent dancer and was quite the catch before marrying Martha Custis. They never had any biological children.

To improve his farming, he experimented with new crops, fertilizers, crop rotation, tools, and livestock breeding. Receiving a donkey from the King of Spain, Washington became one of the first and best breeders of the American mule.

Washington was given the honor of being the first person to sign the US Constitution.

"Religion and morality are the essential
pillars of civil society."

"Drool" ius Caesar

Born: 100 BC, Suburra, Italy
Died: 44 BC, Curia di Pompeo, Rome, Italy

Gaius Julius Caesar took on a lot of roles in a short life. He had been a fugitive, prisoner, rising politician, army leader, legal advocate, rebel, dictator and became the most powerful person in Rome by the end of his life.

He created the Julian calendar, which replaced an earlier Roman calendar that was based on lunar cycles. It has 365 days in each year, divided into 12 months, with an extra day added every four years. The month of July was named after Julius Caesar.

Caesar was captured by pirates in 75 BC, who held him prisoner for 38 days to collect a ransom.

Caesar was elected consul of Rome in 59 BC, which is the highest political office. By 45 BC, Caesar had been appointed 'Imperator', which meant Roman leader for the rest of his life.

In his play, "Julius Caesar", Shakespeare warned, "Beware the Ides of March!" to commemorate the day on which Caesar was killed.

"It is better to create than to learn!
Creating is the essence of life."

"Bark" beard

Born: 1680, Bristol, England
Died: 1718, Ocracoke, North Carolina

Edward Teach (or possibly Thache), known as Blackbeard, was a fearsome pirate who attacked ships for profit.

He served as a Privateer for England, but then, the riches of being a pirate lured him to a life of crime. He commanded a fleet of ships and had a crew of several hundred pirates.

He often put lit matches, or fuses, under his hat to look scary. He grew his black hair on his beard long and made it smoke while he was fighting to strike fear in the heart of all who saw him.

Blackbeard's pirate flag was black with a skeleton holding a spear pointing at a red heart. He also had a famous ship called, *Queen Anne's Revenge*, that had 40 cannons on it, making it one of the most dangerous pirate ships in history.

He died in battle at Ocracoke Island. Blackbeard's crew thought they decimated their foe, but when they boarded the main vessel, they were ambushed by a group of hidden sailors. After a fierce fight, Blackbeard was killed by British sailors.

"Time and tide waits for none!"

Queen Eliza "bark" II

Born: 1926, Mayfair, London, England
Died: 2022, Balmoral Castle, Scotland

Elizabeth Alexandra Mary Windsor was never supposed to be in line for the throne but became, "heir apparent" when her father, Berty, ascended to the throne because his older brother abdicated in 1936.

She became Queen at age 25 and she reigned for over 70 years, which the longest reign of any female monarch in history.

Her nickname was, "Lilibet" and her great granddaughter is named Lilibet Diana after her.

In 1945, Elizabeth and her sister, Margaret, joined the massive crowds, in the streets of London, to celebrate the end of World War II.

She was given her first horse, a Shetland pony named Peggy, by her Dad, the King. Elizabeth also owned over 30 Corgis in the span of her lifetime. She was an excellent dog trainer and animal lover.

Queen Elizabeth opened the iconic Sydney Opera House in 1973.

"Good memories are our second
chance at happiness."

Lud "wag" van Beethoven

Born: c 1770, Bonn, Germany
Died: 1827, Vienna, Austria

Ludwig van Beethoven was a German composer and pianist. His birthdate is not known, but the date of his baptism was December 17, 1770. He remains one of the most admired composers in history. Throughout his lifetime, Beethoven composed 722 musical pieces.

Beethoven was nicknamed, "The Spaniard" because he had dark skin and dark hair.

At the age of 25, Beethoven started going deaf, probably as a result of a childhood illness. He was completely deaf by age 46 and was no longer able to conduct an orchestra. However, he continued to compose until his death in 1827, at the age of 56. During his last ten years, he composed some of the most significant works in his repertoire.

Mozart said of Beethoven: "Keep your eyes on him- someday he'll give the world something to talk about."

"What I have in my heart and soul must find a way out. That's the reason for music."

Leonardo "dog" Vinci

Born: 1452, Anchiano, Italy
Died: 1519, Amboise, France

Leonardo da Vinci was an accomplished musician, scientist, and master painter. He sang, and played the lyre and flute, often for nobility. He had no last name. "da Vinci" simply means, "of Vinci", which is a village near Florence.

He was ambidextrous, which means that he could draw forward and backward with opposing hands simultaneously. Leonardo da Vinci wrote most of his work from right to left.

As a painter, Leonardo naturally took an interest in the properties of light and illumination, but he also used his scientific mind to understand their inner workings. He wrote in one of his notebooks that people perceive the sky to be blue because of the sun's illumination of particles of moisture in the atmosphere.

Some of his ideas led to such inventions as: an underwater breathing apparatus, a life preserver, a diving bell, a pile driver, an armored car, a revolving crane, a parachute, a pulley, a method to concentrate solar power, water-powered mills and engines.

"A clever man without wisdom is like
a beautiful flower without fragrance."

Sacaga "wag" ea

Born: 1788, Lemhi River Valley (Present day Idaho)
Died: c 1812, Kenel (Present day South Dakota)

There is a lot that we don't know about this Native woman, but what we do know is that she was an invaluable interpreter and guide for Meriwether Lewis and William Clark's expedition westward from the Mississippi River to the Pacific Coast.

She was a member of the Lemhi Shoshone tribe, which literally translates as Eaters of Salmon.

Sacagawea gave birth to a son named Jean Baptiste, in February 1805. His parents took him on the expedition when they embarked in April 1805. Clark, called him, "Little Pomp" and eventually became the boy's legal guardian after Sacagawea's death.

She and her husband together, spoke several languages and could negotiate with guides and trappers along the trip. She also used her knowledge of foraging to feed the group, but she also could identify plants that serve a medicinal purpose.

"Everything I do is for my people."

"Pup" Gregory I

Born: Born: Metropolitan City of Rome, Italy
Died: 604 AD, Rome, Italy

Pope Gregory was known for his generosity and he gave everything from money to land to the poor, from donations by the wealthy people of Rome. He believed that the duty of the church was to relieve the distress of the poor.

He penned over 800 letters and was known for his many writings and during his lifetime.

He promoted the Gregorian calendar and founded a system of seminaries. Gregory defined the calendar of festivals and the service of priests and deacons, and strengthened the papacy.

He is known for instituting the first recorded large-scale mission from Rome, the Gregorian mission, to convert the largely pagan Anglo-Saxons to Christianity.

For his steadfast guidance, he is one of the few saints that have been granted the title of the "Great."

"The proof of love is in the works. Where love exists, it works great things. But when it ceases to act, it ceases to exist."

Rosa "Barks"

Born: 1913, Tuskegee, Alabama
Died: 2005, Detroit, Michigan

Rosa Louise McCauley Parks was an American activist in the civil rights movement best known for her pivotal role in the Montgomery bus boycott. Parks rejected the bus driver's order to vacate a row of four seats in the "colored" section in favor of a white passenger, once the "white" section was filled.

Following her famous bus protest, she was arrested, convicted, and fined $14. She also lost her department store job as a seamstress.

In 2005, a new species of spider was named after Rosa Parks, Aptostichus rosaparksae.

She has a bronze statue a seated position and is the first full-size statue of a real woman to be placed in the Capitol Rotunda in Washington D.C.

Bus seats were left empty in New York City, Washington, D.C., and other cities on the 50th anniversary of Rosa's arrest to honor her and the results of her civil disobedience.

“One person can change the world.”

Winston "Fur"chill

Born: 1874, Blenheim Palace, United Kingdom
Died: 1965, London, United Kingdom

Sir Winston Leonard Spencer Churchill was an award-winning author, artist, politician, orator, and war correspondent. Although he was known for his speeches, Winston had a speech impediment which meant he had difficulty pronouncing the letter 's'. He popularized the term, "iron curtain.".

As a correspondent in South Africa in 1899, his armored train was ambushed by Boers. Churchill was captured and sent to a prison camp, which he soon escaped from by scaling the wall.

He was in his 40s before he began painting, but would go on to create more than 500 paintings. Some of his works are in the National Trust Collections.

Winston was extremely accident-prone. As a youth, he suffered a concussion and ruptured a kidney while playfully throwing himself off a bridge. He nearly drowned in a Swiss lake, fell off of horses, dislocated his shoulder while disembarking from a ship in India, crashed a plane while learning to fly and was hit by a car when he looked the wrong way to cross New York's Fifth Avenue.

"You will never reach your destination
if you stop and throw stones at every
dog that barks."

Vincent Van Gogh

Born: 1853, Zundert, Netherlands
Died: 1890, Auvers-sur-Oise, France

Vincent Van Gogh was one of the most important painters of the post impressionist movement and his art is well loved for it's beauty, emotion and color. He struggled with mental illness and remained poor and virtually unknown throughout his life.

Van Gogh was the oldest of six children of a Protestant pastor.

He only sold a single painting during his lifetime and got fired from his first job in an art gallery. Vincent painted an impressive 43 self-portraits, but it was because he couldn't afford a model, not out of conceit.

Starry Night was created in a mental hospital. Although it is considered a masterpiece, he thought of it as a failure.

Van Gogh's success can be attributed to his sister-in-law Johanna, the wife of his brother Theo, who committed herself to ensuring his legacy after his death.

"If one truly loves nature one finds
beauty everywhere."

William Shakes "paw"

Born: 1564, (baptised) Stratford-upon-Avon, England
Died: 1616, Stratford-upon-Avon, England

William Shakespeare was an English playwright, poet and actor. He is widely regarded as the greatest writer in history.

He was one of eight children and his parents almost certainly could not read or write. William was well educated. His wife and children, however, were probably illiterate.

The Globe Theater was his large open air place that allowed anyone to enjoy performances. The poor had the cheaper ground floor tickets with no seating and the rich had higher covered seats, away from the stench of the poor.

He coined a LOT of phrases like:

all that glitters isn't gold	heart of gold
catch a cold	melted into thin air
elbow room	leapfrog
all the world's a stage	wild-goose chase
it's Greek to me	one fell swoop

"Love all, trust a few, do wrong to none."

"James Earl "Bones"

Born: 1931, Arkabutla, Mississippi

In 1969, Jones participated in making test films for the children's education series Sesame Street.

He had a stutter. He began using acting, as well as speaking parts he'd memorized, as a way to help him deal with his speech problem, but it led to his impressive acting career.

He served in the military as an Army Ranger. He was with the 75th Rangers Regiment.

In addition to his success in film and television, James Earl Jones has earned a reputation as a highly respected stage actor, starring in numerous productions on Broadway.

Jones narrated all 27 books of the New Testament in the audiobook, "James Earl Jones Reads the Bible".

Over his career, Jones has won three Tony awards, two Emmy awards and a Grammy award.

"One of the hardest things in life is having words in your heart that you can't utter."

Marie Antoinette

Born: 1755, Vienna, Austria
Died: 1793, Paris, France.

Marie was a fashionista who set trends around the world. The Queen of France was actually born in Austria to the powerful Hapsburg family. She was married at 14 years old to the future King of France, 15 year old Dauphin Louis-Auguste.

She loved drinking chocolate so much that she brought her own chocolatier with her from Vienna to Versailles when she married.

She loved fashion and constantly came up with ideas for new dresses and hairstyles, including a hairdo that added a model of the French warship *La Belle Poule* to commemorate its sinking of a British frigate.

In 1788, the town of Marietta, Ohio was founded and named after the French monarch and even sent her a letter offering the Queen a "public square" in the town.

A diamond necklace scam and flouring her hair during a famine, eventually led to her execution.

"You can be assured that I need no one's guidance in anything concerning propriety."

The Beagles

Formed: 1960, Liverpool, England.
Broke Up: 1974, Disneyworld, Florida, United States

The Beatles, made up of John Lennon, Ringo Starr, Paul McCartney and George Harrison, were the most famous and successful band of all time.

Each of them were under 30 years old when The Beatles broke up and they each went on to have successful solo careers.

The Beatles got the idea for their name from Buddy Holly and The Crickets. Also the 1953 movie "The Wild One", in which Marlon Brando's character refers to his gang as "young beetles".

Originally, they dressed in jeans, cowboy boots and leather jackets, and they had an in-your-face rock and roll attitude. They also liked to eat while on stage. It was their manager who convinced them to clean up their act.

The pine tree planted in memory of George Harrison died because of a beetle infestation.

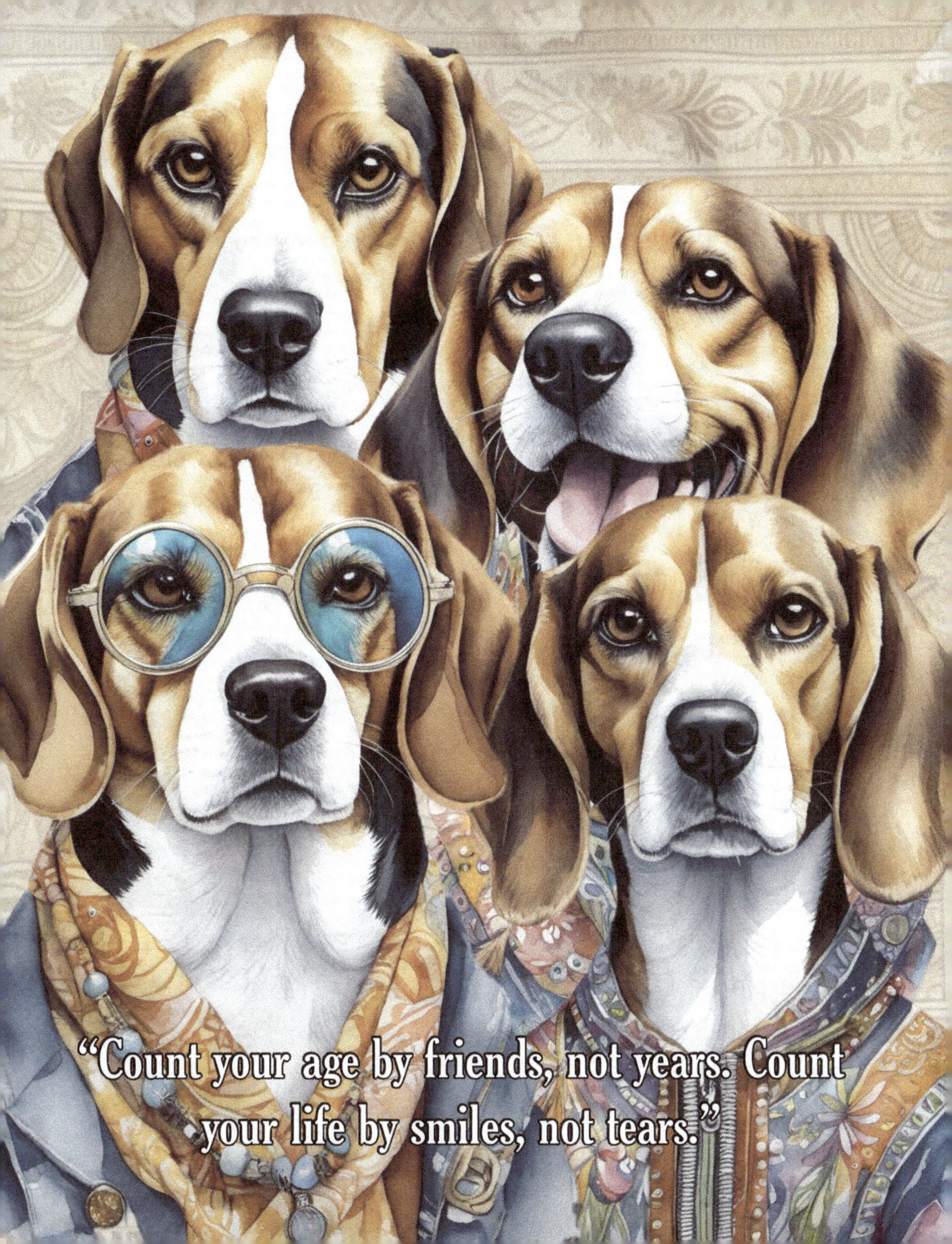
"Count your age by friends, not years. Count your life by smiles, not tears."

Wag of Fame

On the following pages are reimagined real life dog heroes from history. Each of them contributed to humanity in a special way. We do hope that the addition of their protraits in our book will inspire readers to find their stories!

Laika was the first dog in space. The Russians picked the sweet stray to go into space and orbit the surface of Earth in Sputnik II.

Chips was the first dog to receive the Purple Heart and was the most decorated war dog from World War II. He defended and assisted his fellow soldiers.

Apollo was the first dog on site and worked for many 18-hour days to rescue people from the World Trade Towers.

Both were lead dogs that delivered Diphtheria serum in hard conditions in Alaska and saved many lives.

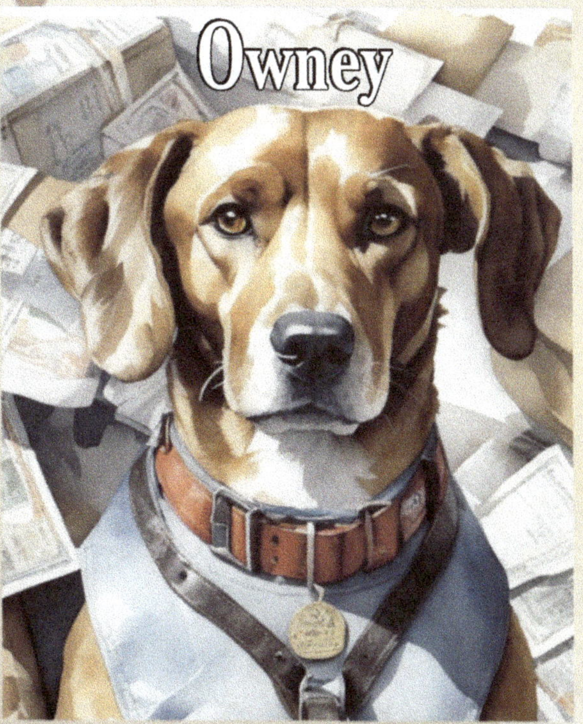

Owney wandered into the Albany Post Office, fell asleep next to the mail bags and never left. He became the Official Mascot of the Rail Mail Service and went all over the world.

Sergeant Stubby

Stubby was smuggled to the trenches of France by his owner and became the most decorated war dog in American history. He even learned to salute with his right paw.

After Mr. Ueno died, his dog, Hachiko, went to the train station to meet him for nine years, proving his extreme loyalty.

Hachiko

Bobby

John Gray's dog, Bobby, showed love for his owner by guarding his graveside for the next fourteen years, until his own death. He is buried in Grayfrair's cemetery, just a few feet from his beloved owner.

Again, Thank you for choosing this book from
Our 3 Sons Publishing.
We appreciate your time in reading our
one-of-a-kind work of art.

We would love to hear what
you thought of this book!
Follow the QR Code to leave
a review. Honest reviews
help readers find the right
book for their needs!